This book belongs to

_____

Walt Disney

VOLUME 1

ALPHABET A-Z

WALT DISNEY FUN-TO-LEARN LIBRARY

A BANTAM BOOK
TORONTO · NEW YORK · LONDON · SYDNEY · AUCKLAND

ISBN 0-553-05501-1

Published simultaneously in the United States and Canada. Bantam Books are published by Bantam Books, Inc. Its trademark, consisting of the words "Bantam Books" and the portrayal of a rooster, is Registered in U.S. Patent and Trademark Office and in other countries. Marca Registrada. Bantam Books, Inc., 666 Fifth Avenue, New York, New York 10103. Printed in the United States of America   0 9 8 7 6 5 4
Classic™ binding
R. R. Donnelley & Sons Company
patents U.S. and foreign pending

Aa

apples

apron

Alice picks apples and acorns on an autumn afternoon and gathers them in her apron.

acorns

Ape-king Louie plays acrobat and just misses an angry alligator.

alligator

ape

"Away we go," says Mickey, as his airplane follows the arrow.

Bb

Baloo the bear has a basket of berries in front and a bee in back.

berries

bear

basket

bee

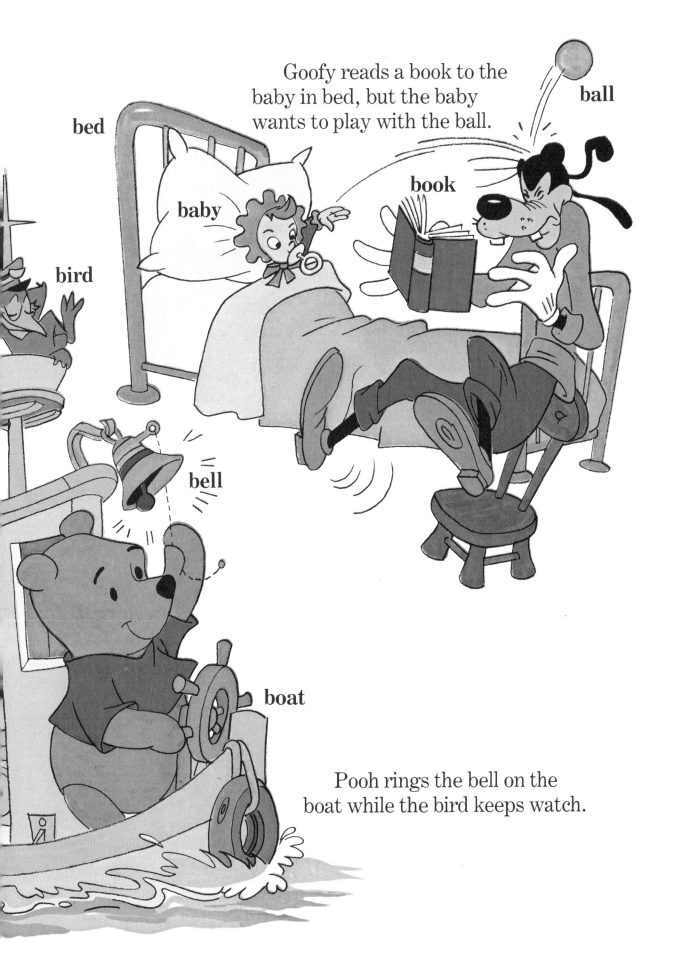

bed

Goofy reads a book to the baby in bed, but the baby wants to play with the ball.

ball

bird

baby

book

bell

boat

Pooh rings the bell on the boat while the bird keeps watch.

Dum-dum-de-dum! Doc plays his drum for a dog, a duck, and a dragon.

Dd

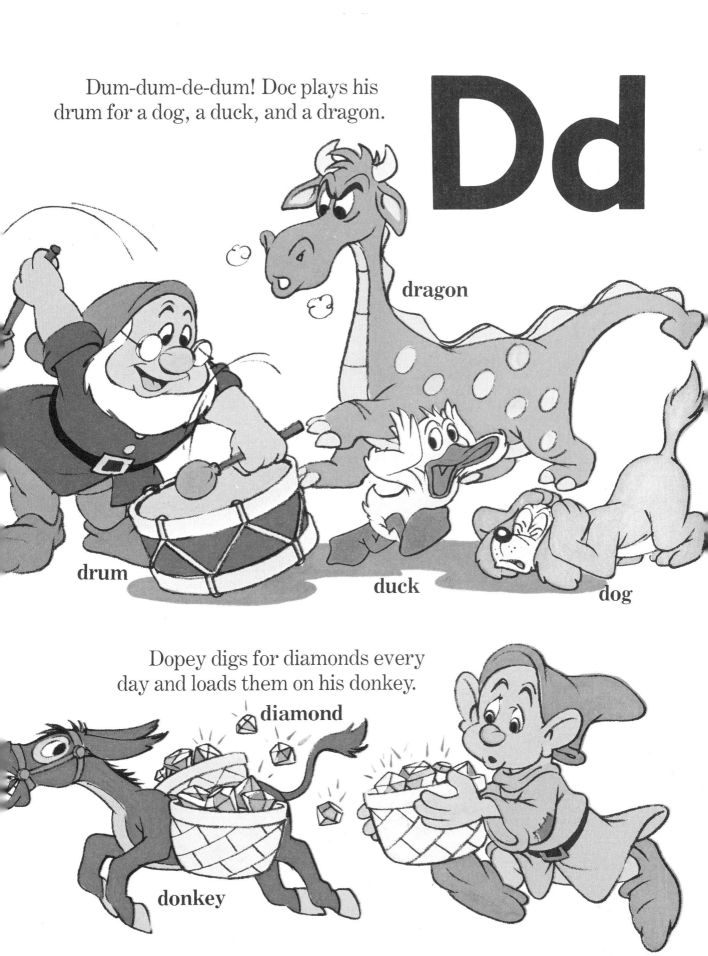

dragon

drum

duck

dog

Dopey digs for diamonds every day and loads them on his donkey.

diamond

donkey

Here are some picture stories. Can you tell what has happened?

A

Say the A words.

B

How many things can you find that begin with B?

C

Say the C words.

D

Say the D words, too.

Ee

ear

Easter basket

eggs

Eeyore's ear tells him he got something extra in his Easter basket of eggs.

Eek! There's an elephant on this elevator! Look out, everybody!

elephant

elevator

elbow

Ff

Foolish Foulfellow the fox hides behind the flowers, but the Blue Fairy finds him.

fence

fairy

fox

flowers

fish

frog

Gg

gate

Grandma Duck gives goodies to the goldfish in her garden pool.

goldfish

garden

Goofy strums his guitar and makes the gorilla giggle.

gorilla

guitar

grass

Captain Hook hangs from a
helicopter high over the housetops.

Hh

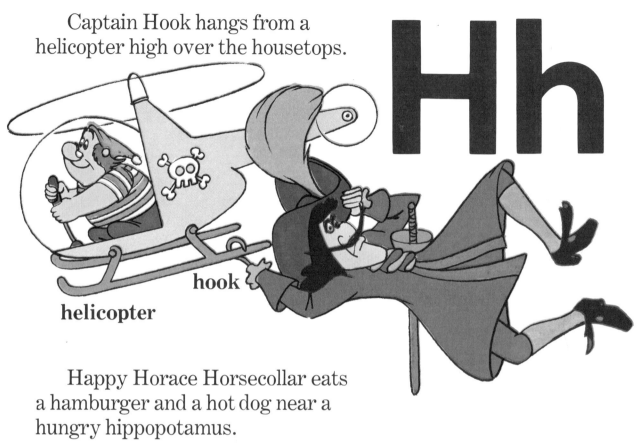

helicopter

hook

Happy Horace Horsecollar eats
a hamburger and a hot dog near a
hungry hippopotamus.

hippopotamus

hat

hot dog

hamburger

Ii

ice

ice cream

ink

Ichabod Crane illustrates I with ice,
ice cream, and ink.

ICHABOD

Jiminy Cricket gets some help from the jack-in-the-box and jumps up to the table where the jelly is.

Jj

jack-in-the-box

jelly

Pinocchio has poured himself some juice from the jug. "Now where's the jelly?" he asks, looking at Jiminy Cricket's jacket.

juice

jacket

jug

JELLY

Here are some more picture stories. Can you tell what has happened?

E

Say the E words.

F

How many F words can you say?

G

Say the G words.

Say the H words
in the picture.

H

Find the I words.

I

J

Find the J words, too.

Kk

Kanga heats a kettle in the kitchen
while little Roo flies his kite.

leaves

Ll

Look out! The lion wants to lick that lemon-flavored lollipop! Louie leaps up a ladder to get away.

ladder

lion

lollipop

Lady brings letters to her lazy friend and lays them on her lap.

lamp

lap

leg

Mm

Mickey Mouse spent his money at the market on milk and mushrooms for supper.

market

money

milk

mushrooms

On the way home he met a magician who changed his milk into a monkey and his mushrooms into a mitten.

monkey

mitten

magician

That night, under a full moon, Mickey sat in a meadow and wondered how it could have happened.

meadow

moon

Nn

No noise in Never Land!
Tinker Bell is napping in a nest
of nuts.

night

nuts

nest

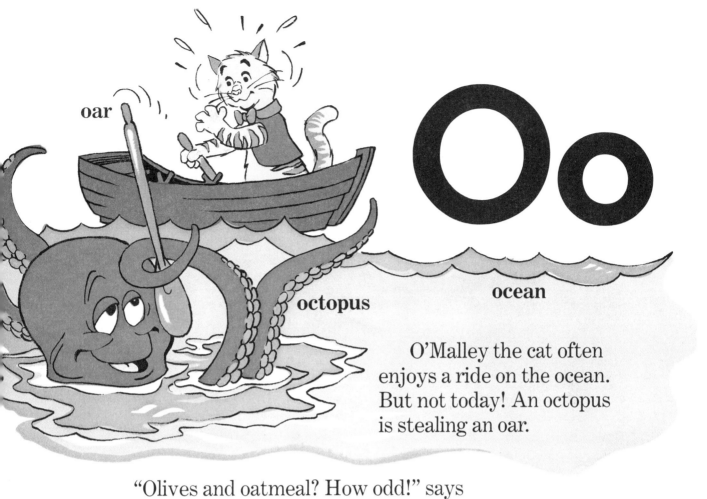

oar

octopus

ocean

Oo

O'Malley the cat often enjoys a ride on the ocean. But not today! An octopus is stealing an oar.

"Olives and oatmeal? How odd!" says Owl to Pooh. "I think I'll go home to my oak tree and have an orange instead."

owl

olives

oranges

P p

While the pirates sleep, Peter Pan looks for things they have stolen. He finds a pencil, a pen, a penny, a purse, a pail, some peaches, and a pumpkin pie.

pirate

pail

purse

pencil

pen

penny

pumpkin pie

peaches

porch

package

puppy

pillow

Pluto and his puppy pal see a package on their pillow. What a pretty present!

pancakes

popcorn

peanuts

Pinocchio paints a picture of his favorite foods — pancakes, popcorn, and peanuts.

Look at the picture stories.
What has happened?

K

Find the K words
in the picture.

Find the L words.

L

M

Say the M words.

N

Say the N words.

Say the O words.

O

Say the P words, too.

P

Qq

queen

The Queen of Hearts
could not find the King.
He was under the quilt,
quietly drinking a
quart of milk.

quart

quilt

Rr

Rabbit has a red raincoat to wear
when he roller-skates in the rain.
Watch out for that rock, Rabbit!

rain

rabbit

raincoat

roller skates

rock

raccoon

rope

roof

Robin Hood climbs a
rope to the roof to rescue a
runaway raccoon.

Ss

"What scrumptious soup," says Snow White, as she stirs in some salt. "Ah-choo!" says Sneezy. Salt makes Sneezy think of pepper, and pepper makes Sneezy sneeze.

salt

spoon

stove

soup

somersault

stairs

Snow White sits on the stairs and watches
Sleepy's super somersault. But he falls asleep!
Sweet dreams, Sleepy.

sky

squirrel

skunk

snow

snake

sled

skis

The skunk on his skis and the squirrels on their sled
make tracks in the snow. "Let me try," says the snake.

Tt

"Look out for the terrible tiger!" calls tiny Tinker Bell as Princess Tiger Lily comes out of her tepee.

tree

tiger

tepee

Tramp the dog finds a tired turtle on the train track and takes it away—just in time!

train

turtle

track

Uncle Scrooge sits under his umbrella and looks at his map of the United States. A unicorn peeks over his shoulder.

Uu

unicorn

umbrella

United States

Here are some more picture stories.
What has happened?

Q

Say the Q words in the picture.

R

Say the R words.

S

Say the words that
start with S.

Say the T words.

T

Find the U words, too.

U

Vv

"Look here," Goofy shouts in a loud voice. "My van is full of surprises." He has a vest for Donald, a veil for Minnie, a vase for Daisy, and a violin for Clarabelle Cow.

van

veil

vase

vest

violin

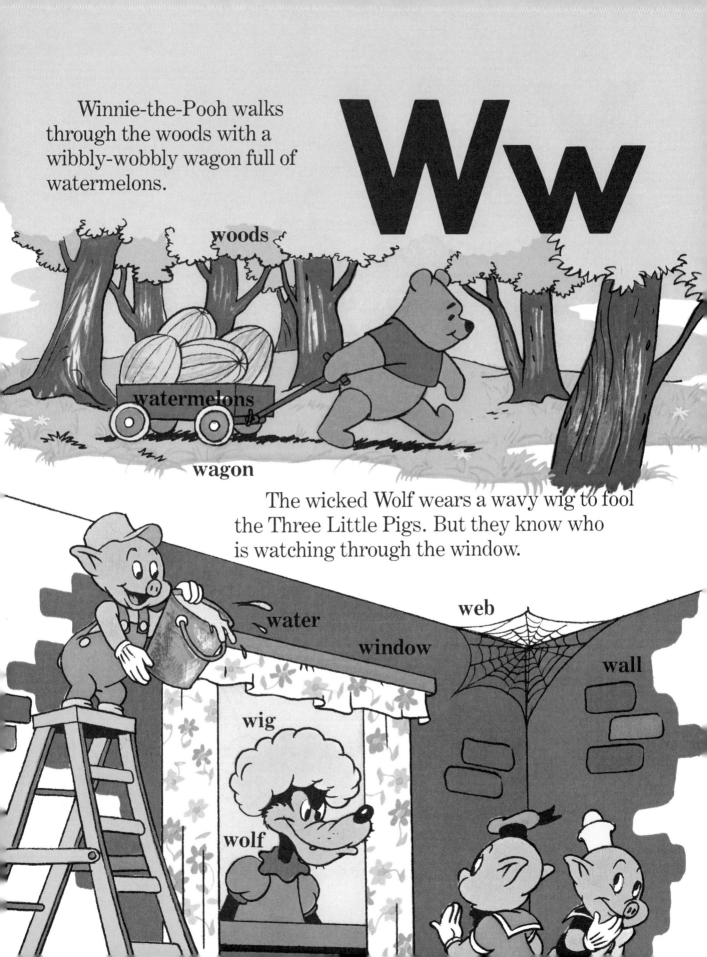

Winnie-the-Pooh walks through the woods with a wibbly-wobbly wagon full of watermelons.

Ww

woods

watermelons

wagon

The wicked Wolf wears a wavy wig to fool the Three Little Pigs. But they know who is watching through the window.

water

web

window

wall

wig

wolf

Xx

X marks the spot on this pirate map. That's where the treasure is.

Pinocchio plays the xylophone while Figaro sings along.

xylophone

"Yippee!" yells Happy. "Watch my yellow yo-yo fly all around the yard!" Poor Sleepy. He yawns and yawns and yawns.

yawn

yo-yo

yard

Yy

Zz

zebra

zoo

"The zany zebra is my favorite animal in the zoo!" says Mickey.

Look at these picture stories. Can you tell what has happened?

V

Say the V words.

Say the W words.

W

X

Can you find an X word?

Say the Y words.

Say the Z words, too.